The Shakespeare Collection

MUCH ADO ABOUT NOTHING

RETOLD BY JAN DEAN

Illustrated by Chris Mould

an imprint of Hodder Children's Books

Character list:

Benedick

Don Pedro
(the prince)

Claudio

Conrad

Don John
(the prince's brother)

Borachio

Hero
(Leonato's daughter)

Leonato

Beatrice
(Hero's cousin)

Ursula
(Hero's friend)

Friar Francis

Constable

Leonato's heart thumped as he ran across the sunny courtyard to the great house, waving a letter in the air. "Great news! The war is over! Don Pedro is coming here tonight!"

Leonato's household buzzed with delight. Don Pedro, Prince of Aragon, here! There would be music, dancing and parties!

*D*on Pedro of Aragon and his men galloped towards the house. Clouds of heat and dust billowed around them. Bright flags flapped in the wind. Beside the prince rode handsome Claudio and clever Benedick. Behind, rode Don John, the prince's brother. His lips were set in a grim line and his eyes were sly.

Everyone went to greet them. At once, Hero, Leonato's lovely daughter, saw Claudio. And Claudio saw her. Somehow Claudio had forgotten just how beautiful Hero was – he'd only thought of wars before.

Leonato bowed to the prince. Don Pedro smiled and shook his hand. Then the whole crowd burst into excited chatter. Benedick began to talk, but only Hero's cousin, Beatrice, looked at him.

"Are you still talking, Signor Benedick? Nobody's listening!"

Benedick pulled a face. "Oh, it's you is it? Miss Mockery!"

Beatrice was lively and funny, but so sarcastic – she never missed a chance to put him down.

"Oh, Beatrice, except for you, all the ladies love me. It's a pity I'm so hard-hearted. I don't love any of them back!"

"That's good news for women. Who'd want you fussing around them? I wouldn't. Like you, I'm hard-hearted. I would rather hear my dog bark at a crow than hear a man swear he loves me!" Beatrice laughed.

Across the courtyard, Leonato was watching Don John, the prince's cold-hearted brother.

Everyone knew he was trouble. He had always been at odds with his brother. In fact he had only recently tried to overthrow him. Now he was sulking because young Claudio had replaced him as his brother's right-hand man.

Leonato stepped towards Don John. "Let me bid you welcome, my lord," he said warmly.

Don John gave a chilly smile, then followed the others into the house for supper.

On their way in, Claudio grabbed hold of Benedick's arm.

"Did you notice Hero – Leonato's daughter?"

"Not specially." Benedick gave him a sideways look. Claudio's eyes were soft and dreamy, like a sick spaniel. Benedick groaned. "I hope you have no plans to turn into a husband! *Have you?*"

Claudio sighed. "I would if Hero would be my wife."

From the doorway Don Pedro called them. "What secret's keeping you from supper?"

Benedick pointed an accusing finger at Claudio. "He is in *l-o-v-e*!" he said in disgust.

Don Pedro gave a knowing smile – he understood what Claudio saw in Hero. Clearly he approved! Benedick did not. "A woman gave birth to me, I thank her. A woman brought me up, I thank her. But I will never be at a woman's beck and call. Benedick lovesick? Benedick the *married man*? Never!"

Don Pedro laughed: "I bet you change your
mind eventually," then turned to Claudio. "Do
you love Hero?"

Claudio admitted it.

"Tonight at the party, I'll pretend to be you
and tell her how you feel," Don Pedro said. "And
then I'll speak to her father for you."

Don John did not go to supper. Happiness did
not suit him. He would not enjoy his stay in this
friendly place. He had only two friends in the
world, Conrad and Borachio, and Borachio
had news.

"A marriage. I overheard Don Pedro promise to be a go-between for Claudio and Hero. Tonight at the party he will court her on Claudio's behalf."

A cunning smile lit Don John's face. His brother, Don Pedro, was very fond of Claudio – in fact, they were best friends. And Don John hated Claudio for getting all the glory in the war. Now he had a plan that could hurt both of them.

The party was fancy dress. The music was loud and the guests had spilled out of the great hall and into the garden. Their costumes were amazing and the masks were wonderful.

Benedick, disguised as a giant, found Beatrice, the milkmaid. She recognized him at once, but pretended not to and still managed to insult him.

"Don't speak to me – I'm *Miss Mockery*, Benedick said so."

"Benedick? Who's he?"

"Oh, just the prince's jester!" Beatrice smiled. Benedick had to either swallow the insult or remove his mask. And Benedick liked to think his disguises were the best. He would hate to be forced to show himself. Whatever happened she had won this round.

Across the garden, Hero was in white with a feathered swan mask. The prince was in green and gold like Neptune. Don John, masked like a jackal, saw Claudio watching them and he seized his chance. Quickly he and Borachio strode towards him.

"Signor Benedick?" Don John asked, though he knew very well that it was Claudio.

Claudio was pleased that his costume had fooled someone. "You know me well," he said. "I am Benedick."

"Don Pedro is in love with Hero. But she's not a suitable bride for a royal prince. You're his friend. Do him a favour. Talk him out of it."

Claudio's head was spinning. Don Pedro in love with Hero? "How do you know this?"

"I heard him swear it was true."

"So did I," Borachio said.

Claudio looked at Hero and Don Pedro. They were smiling and nodding. They looked so happy. It was true. Don Pedro had betrayed him, the prince wanted Hero for himself. Claudio, sick at heart, turned away from the lights and the music and went into the darkness. Don John watched him go and smiled.

Benedick fumed as he told the prince about Beatrice. "She called me the prince's jester. She speaks daggers, every word stabs!"

"Ssh! She's coming," Don Pedro warned.

"Send me on an errand to the world's end!" Benedick begged. "Anywhere to get away from her."

Don Pedro shook his head. He enjoyed watching Beatrice and Benedick make fun of each other. But what was wrong with Claudio? "Are you sad? Sick?"

"Jealous!" said Beatrice.

"Then he's mistaken," Don Pedro announced. "Claudio, Hero is yours. I've spoken to her father for you. Name your wedding day."

"Tomorrow!" Claudio cried.

"Next week," Leonato said calmly. Weddings could not be arranged at a moment's notice.

"Don't worry, Claudio," Don Pedro whispered. "The waiting will not be dull. I have a plan to make Beatrice and Benedick fall in love with each other. Come with me and I'll explain."

In the deep shadows Don John seethed. The wedding was announced – his plan had failed.

"I can stop it," Borachio said slyly.

"How?"

"Hero has a friend, Margaret. And Margaret loves me. She'll do anything I ask. The night before the wedding, I'll tell Margaret to try on Hero's finest dress. When she's disguised as Hero, I'll act out a love-scene in Hero's room, right by the open window...

Bring Don Pedro and Claudio. Let them see
Hero with another man. Trust me, there'll be
no wedding bells."

Don John closed his eyes. It was a cruel joke.
He loved it.

Next day Benedick was lazing in the orchard. All this wedding stuff was getting him down. Why did men make fools of themselves over women? Love-sickness? Huh! Benedick was never going to catch that disease!

"If I meet a beautiful woman, I stay cool. If I meet a clever one, I stay cool. If I meet a kind and good one, I stay cool. It would take a very special woman to make me love-sick. She'd have to be rich, wise, good, beautiful, gentle, a clever talker *and* able to sing and dance. Uh-oh," Benedick rose to his feet and made for the bushes. "Here comes the prince with Leonato and Claudio, *Mr L-o-v-e*. I'm out of here."

Don Pedro saw Benedick hide. He winked at Leonato then raised his voice, making sure that Benedick could hear.

"Leonato, is it true that Beatrice is in love with Benedick?"

Claudio joined in the trick at once. "I never thought that lady would fall in love with anyone!" he declared loudly.

"Nor I," agreed Leonato. "Especially not Benedick – she treats him dreadfully."

"Has she told Benedick?" asked Don Pedro.

"No. And she never will. Hero says that Beatrice is so sick with love that she will die," Leonato replied.

"If she won't tell him, we must let him know," Don Pedro urged.

"No. He'd make a joke of it and torment her. Say nothing," said Claudio.

With that, the three of them went in to lunch, trying not to laugh.

Behind the orchard hedge Benedick was stunned. "Beatrice? In love with me? Ready to die rather than tell me?" He could hardly believe it. Beatrice was a wonderful woman – everything he could want. She was beautiful, good and wise, "—except for loving me," he muttered. Maybe there was something in this love stuff, after all…

"When I said I would die a bachelor," he told himself, "I did not think I should live till I were married…" Suddenly he made up his mind – he would fall *horribly* in love with Beatrice.

In another part of the garden, Hero and her friend, Ursula, were about to play the same trick on Beatrice.

Ursula spoke loudly and clearly. Even though Beatrice was well behind them she was bound to hear. "Are you sure that Benedick loves Beatrice?"

"So say the prince and Claudio. They asked me to tell her, but I said no. There is no woman prouder than my cousin Beatrice. Disdain and scorn sparkle in her eyes. She *cannot* love."

"Sure, I think so, too, but tell her anyway. See what she says."

"No. I'd rather visit Benedick and talk him out of this quite hopeless love."

Out of the corner of her eye Ursula spied Beatrice's shocked face.

"She's hooked!" she whispered.

Giggling, they ran in to lunch.

Beatrice clapped her hands over her ears. "Can this be true? Do they really think me so proud and scornful?" She thought of Benedick. He was attractive and funny. No one else could stand up to her half so well. And he wouldn't bore her to death with silly love songs. Handsome Benedick would make her laugh. "Love on, Benedick," she whispered.

That night, in the shadows under Hero's window, Don Pedro and Claudio stood horrified and amazed. Outlined against the bright light of the room stood a man holding a woman in his arms.

"See!" Don John said.

Claudio stared. That dress… Those jewels in her hair… It was Hero! With a bitter heart, Claudio cursed her.

*T*he next morning, the church glowed with flowers. The scent of lilies drifted in the air. The wedding party gathered at the altar.

The priest smiled at Claudio. "You are here today to marry Hero?"

"No."

Everyone fell silent. *No?* The crowd murmured.

"There must be some mistake," the prince said. He had seen Hero with his own eyes. She was untrue. Not fit to marry Claudio.

Lies! Poor Hero begged them to believe her. She was innocent. But Claudio turned his back on her. Even her father seemed to believe the terrible story. Desperate and trembling with shock, Hero fell into a dead faint.

The guests left quickly, leaving Leonato and his family alone.

"This is some dreadful error," the priest said. "Take my advice, spread the rumour that Hero is dead. Killed by shock and shame. Then Claudio will pity her and wish he'd never said a word. Come, lady," he said, gently leading Hero away.

*B*eatrice wept. She was angry at the lies told about her cousin, sad for her cousin's pain. More than anything she wanted Claudio to pay for what he had done to Hero. Benedick watched her crying. This was no time for jokes or for pretending.

"I love nothing in the world as well as you," he admitted. "I would do anything for you."

Beatrice lifted her head. "Kill Claudio," she said.

Benedick was shocked. "Not for the wide world," he whispered.

"Then you do not love me," Beatrice said, turning away. "If I were a man, I'd do it."

"I do love you," Benedick protested. "If you really want this, I will challenge Claudio." And he went away.

*N*ews of Hero's death soon reached Claudio, but he showed little remorse. He could hardly believe it when good-natured Benedick seemed angry with him and even challenged him to a duel. But before this could happen, there was a disturbance outside the house.

Don Pedro went to investigate. What's this? The local constable and his men with Borachio and Conrad in chains?

"What have you done?"

"We caught them in the night," the constable explained. "Don John's the ring-leader. He's run away, but we'll catch up with him. These two were boasting about a wicked plot against the lady Hero. They tricked Margaret into dressing up as her, while *this* one," said the constable, digging Borachio in the ribs, "kissed her and called her by Hero's name."

Claudio went white. He had wrongly accused Hero. And now she was dead. He fell to his knees before her father, Leonato, and begged forgiveness.

"Choose your revenge yourself," Claudio pleaded, promising to do anything that Leonato asked of him.

"You cannot make my daughter live again –
that is impossible. But you can clear her name.
Tonight at her tomb, sing sad songs to her bones.
And since you cannot be my son-in-law, be my
nephew. My brother has a daughter, almost the
double of my dead Hero. Marry her instead."

Desperate to make amends, Claudio agreed.

The following day four veiled women waited at the church.

"Which is the lady?" Claudio asked.

"This one."

"Sweet, let me see your face."

"No," Leonato insisted. "Not till you take her hand before the priest and swear to marry her."

Claudio knelt and took the lady's hand. "I am your husband," he said.

At this, she lifted her veil.

Claudio gasped.

"Hero?" Don Pedro said, amazed.

It was like magic. All the evil done by Don John was washed away, as if it had never been.

Benedick looked at Beatrice. Weddings were in the air. Happy endings were in order. This was probably a good moment to propose.

"Beatrice, do you love me?" he asked.

She looked at him. Talk of love, in front of all these people?

"Of course not!" she said.

"But the prince said you loved me!" Benedick blurted.

"Well, Hero said you loved me," Beatrice snapped.

"But you don't?"

"No."

"You?"

"No."

"He does. I'll swear it!" Claudio shouted.
"Here's a love poem in his handwriting!"

"And here's another written by my cousin –
I stole it from her pocket!" Hero cried.

Proof. Undeniable proof.

Benedick looked at Beatrice. "I will marry
you," he said. "But only out of pity."

Beatrice looked at Benedick. "Very well, I give
in. But only to save your life – they told me you
were going to die of love!"

"Well, well," Don Pedro grinned. "Benedick
the *married man*!"

Benedick smiled. "Claudio, I planned to kill you for what you did to Hero. Now we are to marry these two cousins, we are family. Friends. Let's have music! Dancing!"

In the middle of the jokes the constable dragged Don John in, a prisoner in chains. But Benedick would not have such a happy day turned sour by thinking about Don John's wickedness.

"Leave him, Prince," he said. "Until tomorrow." The serious business could wait. Now it was time to celebrate. With a great fanfare the band began to play.

"Come on," Benedick cried. "Dance!"

The Shakespeare Collection

Look out for these other titles in the Shakespeare Collection:

Macbeth Retold by Anthony Masters
When Macbeth meets the witches on the heath, he can't believe
the fame and fortune they predict for him. Then he sees that
with one murder it could all be within his grasp.

A Midsummer Night's Dream Retold by Clare Bevan
What happens when the fairy world and the mortal world
collide? Disaster! Demetrius is in love with Hermia, who is in
love with Lysander, who is in love with Helena, who is in love
with Demetrius! Will they ever sort out this mess, or do they
need a little help from the fairies?

Romeo and Juliet Retold by Rebecca Lisle
The Capulets and Montagues have always hated each other, so
when Romeo falls in love with his enemy's daughter, they must
keep their love a secret. If they are discovered it could mean
war between the two families...

You can buy all these books from your local bookseller, or
order them direct from the publisher. For more information
about The Shakespeare Collection, write to: *The Sales
Department, Hodder Children's Books, a division of Hodder
Headline, 338 Euston Road, London NW1 3BH.*